God Always Cares

Coloring Book

Standard
PUBLISHING
CINCINNATI, OHIO

ISBN 0-7847-1452-5

09 08 07 06 05 04   9 8 7 6 5 4 3

God always cares.

"He cares for you." *1 Peter 5:7*

Flowers blooming in my yard,

New leaves budding on my tree;

Those are ways my Father shows

That he always cares for me.

When I gaze at a starry sky,

Or when I play beside the sea,

God is with me all the time

Because he always cares for me.

Dear God, I'm very glad to know

That you are watching over me.

I will trust you all my life

Because you always care for me.

"Your Father knows the things you need." *Matthew 6:8*